time difference
jennifer wong

VERVE
POETRY PRESS
BIRMINGHAM

PUBLISHED BY VERVE POETRY PRESS
https://vervepoetrypress.com
mail@vervepoetrypress.com

FIRST PUBLISHED SEP 2024

Printed and bound in the UK
by Imprint Digital, Exeter

ISBN: 978-1-913917-53-1

Cover Photo by: Sylee Gore

*'I ask T what I should call the thing I write about
Saturation, because she's a titleologist, and she says,
Someplace Like Montana.'*
- 'Someplace Like Montana' - *Ada Limón*

CONTENTS

Acknowledgements

time difference

it's been so long, so long. now, where do we even start? when I last came to visit, where did we go for dimsum?

i'm missing you all and crystal jade xiaolongbao.

charlotte's Mandarin, she draws the characters too, like 日, 月, 人, 窗戶. this week, i'm teaching her all the pronouns and hobbies in my mother tongue.

mum, the virus continues to mutate, and england is still locked in this winter of brexit.

and yes, i'm still a poet. although when i fill in application forms i never mention it, and sometimes i'd choose none of the above. when other parents in charlotte's school ask me, i mumble something else.

i'd like to grow this inside me quietly like a precious seed.

time differentiates us. When we are having our coffee and breakfast pastries, you're already slurping your wonton noodles

often, after dinner, i want to call you but you're already asleep.

i'm baking and the whole house this morning smells of sourdough. i know you'd love that.

mum, one day it'd be great to talk to you about liz berry or victoria chang.

if you'd try and read my poems, you'll find yourself in many of them. mirrors where i look for you.

you might even ask me why, after what seems like a whole lifetime.

from where I live

In 1749, the poet Gotthold Ephraim Lessing commented: "I am going to Leipzig, to a place where one can see the whole world on a small scale."

outside my window,
other windows

stay perfectly upright, perfectly still
wenn die moleküule flimmern

min den zellen die meine gedanken maschen sollen

when we can meet again, we must
go to Kaffeehaus Riquet for the best coffee; you must

visit the lake of tears in front of
the monument of the battle of nations.

ket us stroll down to Nikolaikirche,
where the people's resolve changed our history:

how the wall crumpled like paper, how we
begin again in this city of the artists.
.

when the day comes, we will
argue about Nietzsche:

the difference between gut, schlecht, and böse;
drink, celebrate our friendship.

wenn zwischenn synapsen kurtzschlüsse funken flackern machen

shall we   believe in healing
listen for hope in Wagner's *Ride of the Valkyries*,

or in Mendelssohn's *Songs without Words*
as one day music will return to Oper Leipzig.

in this new quiet, this strange, bird-less winter,
i write my next play:

slowly, gently, i let the sentences arrive;
imagine the stage, the audience, the curtain call.

recipe for becoming your best daughter

Serves 2

Ingredients
2 tbsp of filial piety
3 cloves of calmness
Perfection onions, finely chopped
400g politeness, minced
Chinese logic
salt and proper

Method
1. wake before eight.
2. if it rains, don't go out of house wearing jeans.
3. sit on sofa and watch TV together. resist idea of picking up a book: reading is subversive, antisocial.
4. make yourself useful in the house: wash the dishes, sweep the floor, wipe the walls with clean cloths and fold up the laundry. prepare yourself to be 別人的太太.
5. join mother on her daily trips to the wet market. navigate through the hubbub. visit her favourite grocers: *can you give me a bunch of free spring onions please!* look at the fishmonger, how he flicks off the sequin-like scales from the fish.
6. marry someone Chinese, who lives close to home, preferably in Kowloon (so no cross-harbour travel involved).
7. fingers crossed that he is a doctor or an accountant or some one reliable.
8. don't leave her behind.
9. travel 200g in time and don't resign from that job. take out the suit from the wardrobe you haven't worn for years and put it on. she was so proud of you.

hinterland

day after day you put on weight
and it's harder to type
with one hand, nurse with the other.

how do we dream back
the body we used to wear:
the waist, the supple breasts,

a sensuous ratio of parts.
i have forgotten the joy of gaze,

in the hinterland of giving.
my baby's drowsy eyes close,
the minutes on the clock glide

and i can return to my desk, or acknowledge
that i have been tired for a long time.

the last of everything

if I knew that would be my last afternoon to order a soya latte

the last time i went into M&S to buy a skirt, feeling its rich velvet before deciding

jane and i, we kept talking about meeting up for breakfast, and afterwards we'd go and check out *Titian: Love, Life and Death*

i never realised how much my students meant to me until i stepped into an empty classroom

at the moment my inbox is filled with sincere apologies: *we're sorry the world is no longer as you recognise it*

memories of Tuesday afternoons: school foyer packed with all the daughters fitting into tutus and ballerina flats

that pitch dark evening walking to the train station

talking like we'd always do, a simple goodbye hug. my last chance to

followed by years of disproportionate disappearing

i don't want to think about the gorgeous, useless bouquets at Waitrose on Mother's Day: all the grandmothers who stayed at home in their best clothes, ready to skype

the day before the lockdown, our children were at the local park. all they could play was the seesaw. one on each side, two metres apart

komorebi

is a language of shadows, as in it
all lies in how it was meant and
translated, not what was said. In
the colour of a fired pot. strong
tiger leaves. In the slowness of
your voice, each word gaining
weight, despite all unlikelihood.
In the komorebi as we talked.
walking in circles as if the
afternoon or the quad of our
selves will never end, the wind
breathing down our shoulders as
if worried what the paper cups
might hold. Should I go back to
the simpler questions, as in try to
understand who you were before
we met? Is there anything waiting
for me by the time we reach the
next fountain or tree or bench?
Freedom is the best gift you can
give to anyone. But I'm still
listening for the faintest hint.

Sitting in the car with my brother as he drove me through the slate-grey streets from Tsim Sha Tsui to Prince Edward on a Monday morning, somewhat cloudy, before leaving home once again

as we watch the worker in front of your car
loading and unloading boxes.
you've stopped by a Pret

so I could get my coffee, the westerner in me
craving what you do not. you said
you've decided

that you wouldn't leave.
not yet. we've got to
love what's still there.

next year, your son would go
to your old 母校.

i asked if you feel that things
are much changed now.
which newspaper should I read?

 you shifted gear,
drove on,
& it started to rain.

Alexa, is yoga the best way to lose weight?

Should I dye my hair?

When can I travel to Argentina, to see the waterfall?

It's been two whole months since I sent my poems to *POETRY* and I've not heard back.

Alexa, the other day, my boyfriend—the one I watched *Joker* with—said that he wished I wasn't Chinese.

Look at Cate Blanchett at the Oscars: her voice, her sunshine face.

Alexa, did you like ballet when you were young? When I was a kid I had always wanted to, but thought we were too working class.

I cannot believe that Taylor Swift has so many followers.

Alexa, teach me how to make California rolls.

Alexa, Alexa, these days I have trouble falling asleep, and often wake up in strange hours, thinking of the bad dream on repeat: words that got trapped in my throat,

please   what should I do   with my heart

婆婆

in my mind i would carry you, because you have tiny
feet. i'd carry you to eat the best fish and chips in town.
make you dumplings in my new home: you'd cluck
your tongue because the dumpling skin would be far
too thick. we would laugh at the way the gwailos hold
their chopsticks. you'd be shocked to see a girl with
tattooed arms wearing a flimsy dress on the coldest
night. you won't believe how the westerners risk their
lives drinking water straight from the tap, how they
don't get sore throats munching whole bags of Kettles
crisps. i would carry you to see Big Ben, turn the clock
backwards like Mary Poppins. we would travel to
Diagon Alley, where Harry and Hermione will greet
you with their owls. i would carry you to Hyde Park,
where you will feed your first swan. your body will
regain strength as we ride an ombre-pink, sheepskin-
soft rickshaw to cross the Thames, feeling triply
young, singing 茉莉花 in the river breeze

Streetside pingpong and hotpot nights once upon a summer

in mongkok or / 'crowded corner' /
where young people go / looking
for sticker cards of celebrities / the
spiciest fishballs / buying web
cameras and iphones / from 信和/
you are one of them / wading
across an ocean / to cross
these streets / know that a
red minibus means speed /
or danger / the old man
sells / sunkist oranges &
bananas / & on a seasonal
basis / dragon-fruit or
long-yan / or 光蘇餅 /
reads 馬經 for betting tips /
no, there's no garden in Fa
Yuen Street / and round the
corner / the trendiest
people you can spot /
wearing cropped tops and
the wildest dreams / as they
fill the entire 波鞋街 / they
used to look forward to /
hotpot dinner gatherings /
in times of peace / you were
one of them / wading across
this ocean / humming / the
song you sang / not so much
about 八珍甜醋 / but grief / &
seeds

between us

under the canopy of the chestnut tree, we asked each other about our childhoods, and i told you my love for the anime *I Love Cream Marron*, how beautiful she is when she transforms herself into a purple-haired singer with her magic pouch.

the other day, you texted me saying, just checking in to see how you are, sent me photos of jamie playing obstacle race in the garden.

pigeons pecking on the grass. two bigger boys comparing their Pokemon cards in the playground.

in our local park, you talked about the days you studied at Guildhall, when you dreamt of becoming an actress. all the odd jobs you did back then to get by. every part you auditioned for: from a village baker in the local pantomime, to Anna in *The King and I*.

i loved it, every moment on the stage.

one night you taught me how to map out the furthest stars with 'Star Walk', your phone a planetarium glowing in the dark.

late

'look at the old house in the dawn rain / all the flowers are forms of water'
- from WS Merwin's 'Rain Light'

you never saw what I saw

        on the day of the downpour

                your hair matted with rain

                    the dog-eared books you've been
                    holding for a while getting soaked

the other day, we stood

      in a fully-packed train carriage, talking about

        The Lateness of the World

one winter morning we walked to a cafe, the day was

              icy cold   hands in pockets, i steered

my attention

         in the direction of   fresh croissants and skinny lattes

sometimes, i wished to explain

(but she never replied)

(i didn't want to)

             except that time, time

is slipping away

        & i tried to tell you

as soon as i could

women at the onsen

after Carl Randall

i.
purity in a valley,
purity in a lake.

a world in silhouettes and stillness;
the shape of water in a wooden pail.

ii.
nothing exists beyond the neck,
the shoulder blades, and
a neatly-folded towel on the head.

iii.
the women fled the glass tower
and all those smiles in Ginza.

what's left are just limbs,
secrets shrouded in steam.

in order to arrive at
the lake: its utopian
blue and amnesiac.

iv
beyond the small ryokan
the black mountains stare
at a few bare torsos.

butterflies in the dark.

kinder to self

i would rather have sent you
a postcard of a picturesque
childhood or a caramel heart

but instead all i sent was a
gold-embossed paper crane
with cherry blossomwings

its bent Chiyogami neck
looked as if it were
searching for life's rich nectar or

shying away from its tough questions.
memory: a clock with eager hands
pointing forever towards

forgive, forgiveness:
the bluest lake of time
in a dreamed up hour.

Say somewhere in norwegian wood someone

looks out of a window and their world
is no longer the same

> in those shards of sunlight   you
> notice a beautiful cobweb

> (in the crowd you hear the name,
> you were holding a glass of martini with an olive floating in it
> & don't know how to react)

say somewhere in the novel, someone will die,
out of thirst or
out of love, and you cannot help them.

> in the room the tulips are
> wilting, though no one sees

> as we continue to walk in circles

> & there's the fog, the farm, the sheep
> giving birth

& somewhere another morning of beijing,
the people in Friendship Plaza
are doing their taichi, & hear distinctly

> the sounds from
> the bell tower and the drum tower

& somewhere in time, you
were convinced that the world is good.

Houhai

You asked about water, and this is the water I think about:

The glow of myriad colours on the lake at night. Rickshaw drivers practising their English consonants and vowels with tourists as they pedal past the hutongs, earning five yuan each time—not even a pound.

When Kublai Khan first arrived in Beijing, they called this lake hai —sea—for they have lived all their lives in the desert, and would not have seen much of a sea.

A mesmerising stretch of water from Di An Men all the way to Xin Jiekou and Pingan Dajie.

And the palace, so far away.

From there you can see Prince Chun Mansion where the father of Emperor Puyi was born.

Its season of lotus flowers and pristine snow.

The smell of Xinjiang style lamb skewers and pork belly, cooked halal tripe, fried sausages, the bicycle bells, the songs from the bars.

The workers have such tanned faces and broad shoulders. Students who frequent here after their classes. Couples who fall in love.

Those who come here out of a nameless sorrow, who cannot speak, and long to be healed by the sea.

And the photo we took at Silver Ingot Bridge.

What has become of this country?

The dust, even the dust, seems affectionate.

And if someone were to whisper to me, Shíchàhài, I can feel the restless breeze of history rippling again in the air.

ACKNOWLEDGEMENTS

Thank you to editors who have published these poems in magazines: 'from where I live' was commissioned for Stanza Poetry Festival's digital Window-Swap project (2021); 'amniotic' (originally titled 'umbilical') in *Tentacular, issue 8* (2021); 'Mongkok, or 'Crowded Corner'' in the online project Singapore-HK Travel Bubble project (January 2021); 'As Mother' in *Poetry Wales 57.3* (2022) and 'Recipe to be the kind of daughter she would approve of' in *Poetry Wales 58.1* (2023); 'between us' in *Signalhouse edition issue 22* (2023) and *The Abandoned Playground* (2022); and 'Sitting in the car with my brother' in *Where Else: An International Hong Kong Poetry Anthology* (Verve Poetry Press, 2023); Fragments of 'Kinder to self' in *State of Play: Poets of East and Southeast Asian Heritage in Conversation* (Outspoken Press, 2023); '婆婆' in *The Oxonian Review* (June 2024); 'Houhai' in *Wasafiri* (March 2021); 'Alexa' in *Seisma Magazine* online (Winter 2023).

Thanks to Stuart at Verve, Jacqueline Saphra, Kit Fan, Laura Jane Lee, Oxford TORCH and the Society of Authors.

ABOUT THE AUTHOR

Jennifer Wong was born and grew up in Hong Kong, has a PhD in creative writing from Oxford Brookes University. She is the co-editor of *Where Else: An International Hong Kong Poetry Anthology* (2023) and is the author of *Home, Identity and Writing Elsewhere* (Bloomsbury, 2023).

Tapping at Glass
by *Tim Tim Cheng*

Tapping At Glass charts girlhood, multilingualism, and psychogeography from Hong Kong to Scotland. Myths, meditations on the arts and mass media, and migration stories entwine. Through protest-stricken urban spaces, love hotels, farming as activism, frog watching, alternative therapies, and seascapes where racial and social memories flow in all directions, the working class subjects in Cheng's poems reflect on what it means to exist in one locale and dream of elsewhere, where the past and future, interconnectedness and othering, are in perpetual negotiation. Tapping into various moods, Cheng's poems question the making of a self and a city, and the languages one uses to translate microhistories

"Tim Tim Cheng is a wonderful new voice in the poetry landscape. Playful, serious, complicating any attempt to pin her down – even in the short span of a pamphlet she dances through images and ideas. Already so accomplished, she is definitely a poet who is going places." - Niall Campbell

Available in paperback:
ISBN: 978 1 913917 29 6
48 pages • 210 x 148 •31 poems
£7.99

And on eBook:
ISBN: 978 1 913917 77 7
£5.99

Where Else:

An International Hong Kong Poetry Anthology

With an introduction from the editors Jennifer Wong, Jason Eng Hun Lee & Tim Tim Cheng

Featuring both established and emerging Hong Kong poets across generations and continents, this unique anthology offers a glimpse into an exciting, diverse range of voices that make up the diasporic imagination of the contemporary Hong Kong poetry community. Adopting a diasporic approach, the anthology encompasses both native Hong Kong writers as well as expatriate and mixed-race voices who were born or have lived in the city.

'We are Hong Kongers to the core and will defend our cantankerous vivid imagination against all invaders and occupiers. Our poetry is the ultimate expression of freedom and is a harbinger of all that is wondrous!' - Marilyn Chin

Available in paperback:
ISBN: 978 1 913917 36 4
252 pages • 216 x 138 • 106 poems
£14.99

And on eBook:
ISBN: 978 1 913917 79 1
£9.99

ABOUT VERVE POETRY PRESS

Verve Poetry Press is an award-winning press which focussed initially on meeting a local need in Birmingham - a need for the vibrant poetry scene here in Brum to find a way to present itself to the poetry world via publication. Co-founded by Stuart Bartholomew and Amerah Saleh, it now publishes poets from all corners of the UK and beyond - poets that speak to the city's varied and energetic qualities and will contribute to its many poetic stories.

Added to this is a colourful pamphlet series, many featuring poets who have performed at our sister festival - and a poetry show series which captures the magic of longer poetry performance pieces by festival alumni such as Polarbear, Kevin P. Gilday and Imogen Stirling.

The press has been voted Most Innovative Publisher at the Saboteur Awards, and has won the Publisher's Award for Poetry Pamphlets at the Michael Marks Awards.

Like the festival, we strive to think about poetry in inclusive ways and embrace the multiplicity of approaches towards this glorious art.

https://vervepoetrypress.com
@VervePoetryPres
mail@vervepoetrypress.com